Never Give Up

Connect the Dots

Leroy Colley Jr.

authorHOUSE®

AuthorHouse™
1663 Liberty Drive
Bloomington, IN 47403
www.authorhouse.com
Phone: 1-800-839-8640

First published by AuthorHouse   3/25/2010

ISBN: 978-1-4490-9792-9 (e)
ISBN: 978-1-4490-9791-2 (sc)

Printed in the United States of America
Bloomington, Indiana

This book is printed on acid-free paper.

This book is dedicated to my daughters Danielle and Lauren, Late Mother, Luema (Pat) Colley, and my Dad who fought for Blacks in the city of Maple Heights, and all the Children of Maple Heights Schools, who were told there were no money for books

Most of us don't get involved with what is going on in our schools, or city, until something bad happens to our children. My journey started when my oldest daughter was in the fifth grade and continued for years thereafter.

One day my wife and I noticed our oldest daughter would come home withdrawn and at times shaking her leg, when we questioned her about her day, we were shocked to hear her say that it was her teacher that was bothering her.

He sent a letter home one day (marked in red) that stated he was frustrated in trying to teach her. At that point we set up a meeting with him. That's when my quest really started, after the meeting things got worse with the teacher and my daughter, he would throw her book bag in the garbage can, among other things and one day after talking to our daughter she came home and said,

"I had a good day". We asked why so good today, "Because I am in another class room." I was moved to a new class room. Well after investigating the move the next school day, we found out that the teacher had put our daughter in an inclusion classroom with troubled students, without our knowledge. First of all you have to be tested, which by the way was not done. This was done because he wanted her out of his room.

We took this problem to the principal who a that time was the first African American principal. She set up a meeting with all of us and in the meeting she suggested that he could have handled things differently. He told her that was too bad and that he would do it again. My wife and I asked her to have our daughter removed from his class room and put into another. We were allowed at that time to talk to other teachers. After finding a teacher that we thought would be good for our daughter, we wrote a letter to the Principal, and sent a certified letter to the Superintendent and all the school board members (to which this day 8 years later was never answered by the Superintendent or school board member.) The Principal did receive a letter from the Superintendent stating the move was approved, but she was to word her letter to us in such a way that the move was suggested by them and not us.

The Principal had her share of problems which I will explain later. Shortly after the move we became very involved in PTA, school board meetings, and city council, as you will see this became an uphill battle. In May of 1996, I contacted the United States Department of Education.

Now our youngest of two children started having problems. She came home one day crying and said she got a 'C' on her book report when checking with the teacher, she said I looked at it and it looks like she copied it. Thank God we had taken her rough draft with us, when she looked at it we told her our daughter put a lot of time and effort into her work. She changed her grade to a 'B'. She had not even read her report. She asked us what grade do you want me to give her. Keep in mind this was the same teacher I saw one day yelling at a student and putting her finger in his face and the little boy said to her, "You yell at me every day. I can't do anything right, let you tell it". I could go on and on but I won't. I am sure you get the picture of some of the things that go on in some schools.

Now back to the Principal. She was told about wearing her braids and how she dressed at times (African clothing). One day someone told the Principal that the Superintendent said we our not going to renew that Nigger's contract. Keep in mind that the city we live in is fairly small which had a student population at the time of about 3,000 students and the city is divided east side, west side, in which the west side was mostly white populated. Out of 3,000 students, roughly 1,000 were African American. 500 were the other descent, and the rest were White students.

Now after the Principal's contract was not renewed for 'no reason', she sued the school district and actually lost her case. It was because of this case and a lot of other things, that I became known to the TV news media and radio and papers, as the "Activist". To the school board, I became known as "The Trouble Maker". Well I call it being a 'chip off the old block'. My dad was one of the first Blacks in the city who was the cause of Blacks getting jobs in the city. Up until then the only jobs Blacks held were walking behind the garbage trucks. We still as of today only have three (3) Black policemen, no Black firemen, and up until about 3 years ago, no Black men or women on the City Council, and until about eight years ago, only one Black person on the school board, and she was appointed by the Board.

I realize that I wanted to make a difference. I wanted to help people and children get the best education possible so I went to work even harder on stopping corruption, and helping people. We all had a problem with this school system of which I had graduated from in 1973 at that time the system was 3rd from the top of the list in schools now it is 3rd. from the bottom of the list, and on academic emergency.

I realized it was time for a major change if someone did not get involved, but sometimes getting involved can cost you a job, a marriage, your children suffer and even possibly your life, but someone has to do it to make things better, so you pray and stay firm to the end. In a city that was becoming 80% African American, if we did not get some Black guidance counselors, Black school board members, and get rid of some of the 'old regime', and money hungry wolves, that were bringing this school system down to its' knees, our children would not have a chance to survive. This is when I contacted the United States Department of Justice, voting section.

This quest took a lot of time and money. Along the journey I ran into three key people, one of which became a city council person, the other was a former assistant Superintendent, and the third was a school teacher. In this quest for justice and fairness, we all became good friends, and remained friends until this very day.

The first person had her share of problems with the school and her three children. The second person was at one point the assistant Superintendent, personal Director, for our schools. The third person was brought to me after reading what I was doing in the paper and hearing me speak at a meeting. By the way the second person is no longer (by choice) employed with the school district because he did not want to be involved in the corruption.

Let me point out that you must do your homework and get all the answers, and connect the dots, before you start a quest in bringing down a system or any big entity, that is involved with the 'cesspool'. The FBI was contacted at this point with information we had gathered in respect to the school Board's attorney, and the school Board's President. The Superintendent was getting out of hand. Some compared him to 'Hitler'. The school board officials and attorney were milking the system, doing the school Board members favors and giving out contracts to relatives and friends of the school Board members. They were asking for a levy to pass for more money, and the teachers were getting treated very badly by the administrators and most of all the children were suffering.

I started having more meetings in our home, churches, and libraries, for other parents to see and give ideas of how to stop these problems, but we kept running into a dead end. Most people did not want to get involved because if you did, the school Board and attorney would go after you and try and hurt you, or even have you jailed, if possible, a tit for tat.

One instance was a lady whose daughter questioned something a teacher said about sex. The person at that time was elected to city council. She was attacked by the school's attorney, at a meeting for the public, with her credit history put on a table for all to see. Another example is a book by Robert Cormier, <u>The Chocolate War,</u> was made mandatory to read, by my daughter's teacher. My daughter came home after we bought the book and said, "Dad, Mom, I do not want to read this book. It talked about sex and used curse words and talked about jacking off in a toilet." I went to the school and asked if there was another book she and others could read. Keep in mind if children used some of these same words or did these acts, according to the rules of the school, they would be expelled from school.

I took this to the media. This story about this book aired on all three of our local news TV stations for three days in a row. At one point some libraries were trying to get the book off their shelves.

The list of things go on and on of parents and students confrontations. One day a child that we used to watch after school, came to me and said that he had a bad day and that he did not want to 'do that ever again', and started crying. I said, "Do what again"? He said, "He had to clean a toilet with a tooth brush and the Principal made him do it" (By the way this was not the same Principal that was let go. This was her replacement.) The little boy's parents were informed and she asked for help from us because she had talked to the Principal and got no where. We helped her take the facts and story to the media and ended up getting lots of help. By the way, the child had only picked up a Christmas ornament that had fallen off of the tree and put it in his pocket and was giving it to the teacher. The Superintendent made a statement on TV that it was good old fashion discipline.

It had now gotten so bad that when we went to the school board meetings to ask questions, we had to write our questions down, and then hope that you were called and if you were called, you only had three minutes to speak and were being clocked with a stop watch, by the school Board Treasurer, and video taped. You were cut off and thrown out if you said something that the Board did not agree with, or if you called them on the carpet, in any way. The Board's attorney was at every meeting, which was very unusual for districts in this county.

Our school district had the highest rate of African American suspensions and expulsions. They had out dated learning materials. The class sizes were very large, and were using outdated books.

I went every where to get these problems addressed with city officials. I even went outside our city to other city officials, but got very little help. We called and traveled to Columbus, Ohio where I met with public officials of the state and state school board, on many occasions. I explained all of the problems, took all of the documentation, news articles, which had been written, but was told that their hands were tied. We were told, the school can make their own policies and regulations. I went to the United States Department of Education in May of 1996, and after hearing my story, and talking to us in July 1996, they determined that the allegations of disability were true, and we did have a case. Ultimately the only thing the school got was a slap on the hand and a book on policies.

I called Washington DC and contacted an attorney with the United States Department of Justice Civil Rights Division (voting section). After talking with one of their attorneys, in August 2001, they sent in a team of attorneys from Washington DC, who met in my home, with me and had me set up a meeting with the parents, teachers and principals. All of the news media were contacted about the federal government being here. There was a big problem according to the Feds. All hopes and dreams were fading fast. I stared praying even harder. All of our groups and people have lost all hope. It was down to just my wife and I and I could tell even she had lost all hope.

I had given the media so many stories, so I sat down and thought of all the stories I had given the media. They had to investigate. They would not write or air them if they were not true.

It was so bad here that when I called I almost had a direct line to a reporter. That is how hot it was getting here. Reporter after report said we know that something is there, but we just cannot put our finger on it, missing money, over paid attorney, parents, and kids being mistreated, and withholding public records, when we asked for them. Even some reporters were taken off stories

if they got too close to the problems

Studies and comparisons were done finding out that our system had the highest suspensions and expel rate of all school districts and that our school board attorney was making a million dollars a year and was the highest paid school attorney around and was in two other school districts, and maybe more. It was becoming more apparent to me that the attorney was the main source of our problems.

Well the four of us said we are on our own. We set up a web page and started one by one, investigating backgrounds, looking at the history of the Superintendent, Board members, Treasurer, and especially, the Board's attorney and school Board President.

We found out that the school Board President and Superintendent were being run by the attorney, which had major ties to the county. So how do we stop them, by exposing them one by one and hope that people will see the truth.

After some time of investigating and getting records and some contracts, we found that friends and relatives, of school Board officials, had been hired. The school Treasurer had been involved in a scandal in another school district, which had lost over 250 million dollars. The attorney, who represented him at the time, was now our school Board attorney, who brought the Treasurer to our district. Smells fishy, doesn't it? Well, earlier I told you about the one African American that was appointed to the school board, here is how that went.

I was trying to get Blacks elected to seats on the school Board, one person that was on the school board, left because of some money trouble. He was in office and was forced off his seat, which left an opening before elections. I pushed for an African American. Three African Americans applied for that position, along with other people. The Board said that they could not make the decision of whom to appoint, so they sent it to court for an outside judge to decide. Out of all the candidates, one African American woman was chosen, but here is the kick in the butt. She worked with the school Board president on their everyday job with the County and was friends.

The school Board were questioned about this and said they had no qualified candidates! At least one of the persons who applied was a teacher, and one was an attorney, and one was an administrator, but none of them were qualified for helping the good old boys syndrome. Their candidate even made a statement in a local news paper that she had no experience. They just needed someone to go along with the plan, and vote their way for contracts. As time went on the candidate was the subject of talk. She had been cashing her dead mother's social security checks. After some investigating into this we found this was not her first brush with the law, she had been convicted before, for forgery. She should have been released of her seat right away, but this did not happen. Instead they praised her and made her Vice President of the school Board. This was a slap in the face to the parents and children. What kind of message does this send to our children? She went to court and received a slap on the hand.

A reporter that had been following our problems said he was starting to connect the dots we had told him about. The school board President works for the County Auditors office and was his right hand person. The Vice President also works for the County Auditors office. The school Board President's boss had given her big dollars for elections whereas, we found out they spent more time and money to get some of these people back in office, than the seat they were running for, paid per year. Why is that? I will tell you why, they have to keep the crooks in office.

Back to 'connecting the dots', the school Board President was allegedly sleeping with the school Board attorney. The attorney had brought in the Treasurer and so on. Friends and family were on the payroll, like one big happy family.

The four of us, again started holding public meetings and informing the parents of all the wrong doing and exposing all the bad things with proof in writing. The TV and news papers were doing stories every two weeks. It seemed like in investigating our stories and finding out that we were right and that the problems were even worse and deeper than anyone thought.

The schools needed a levy passed. We were not against the levy, but we stated at the meetings that the levy should not pass until we voted in a new school Board. The attorney and Superintendent are appointed by the school Board. The teachers were at a point that a strike was inevitable. We talked to the teachers and the union President. The teachers now voted to strike and stand up to the real trouble makers and to stand behind us and us behind them.

A web site was set up and a petition drive to remove the Board and Superintendent. The web site was set up so the people and kids had a place to express and vent. This site got over 10,000 hits a day from all over. It also brought us some much needed help from outsiders.

A party from another school district got in touch with me to say that the attorney was into their school district and was robbing them blind also. The attorney we found was in another district also robbing them. It was becoming very apparent that the attorney was the biggest problem of all and the school board President was the next problem. They had to go if this school system stood a chance.

During this quest many teachers lost jobs, people got hurt and many wounds needed to mend. At one point, my wife was running for City Council and the school Treasurer tried to say we had taken

$5,000 from PTA. This was a ploy to get us off their trail.

The teachers strike was the largest and longest of any schools in Ohio. It lasted 63 days. Over 2,000 people came out to sign the removal petition. We had to go to the ALCU attorneys to help us in court with a ruling in regards to the removal petition, of which we ultimately won. Also it was election time for 3 of the 5 school Board seats. The push was on. This strike got pretty bad. At one point, the Principal was sent a raccoon head, during the strike. (This Principal died in 2009 at age 48)

The strike made every headline. Teachers from other districts supported and helped with it. The students even walked out of school to protest and wanted their teachers back. The district even hired an outside company that looked like 'Men in Black' to video and intimidate all of the teachers.

After a long and hard strike it ended. The teachers that helped out went back to work without a contract. They turned their attention to the election.

This was the chance of a life time, time to right a wrong, time to change a city school that had not had a change in 30 years. It was time to vote. An all out attack was put on by all of us, the teachers, and outside help from other cities, politicians, mayors, and parents. Not only was it time for elections, the levy was up. Well you might have guessed, three new board members got elected and the levy passed.

But it was not quite over yet. The old school Board and attorney tried to find a way to stop one of the persons who was elected to a seat by saying her day job was a conflict of interest. But God is good. This was over ruled and she took her seat in office (by the way she was a former school teacher of our district which taught my oldest daughter and she is African American). The other two parties were African American who both had children in the district.

After their swearing in ceremony, the first order of business was to 'fire' the attorney. This was the biggest school board meeting ever. The crowd cheered, clapped, and screamed when this was done. (Remember under the old we could not speak. People were put out of the meeting by way of police). Now new rules were set. The public can speak with no time limit. A new law firm was put into place. (The main attorney passed away on September 4, 2006)

Shortly after the school board Superintendent retired. What a happy day! The new Board has levy money. Things are getting better. The rapport is much better. But Rome was not build in a day. New books are being bought; new schools are in the works to be built, starting in 2010. Needed work is getting done and the city officials are working with the school board to help the school system to go in the right direction. The days of no books, spending our money on trips, personal property, and robbing the school districts of money, looks to be over.

The FBI in 2008, states that they have been investigating county officials, which include judges, lawyers, elected officials and businesses. On or about June 2009, Federal indictments started to come down. Some of these included many of the people and companies I gave to the Feds, when I contacted them 6 years ago. This is the biggest bust that I know of ever, which includes many big officials. This was so far wide spread that it is still on going in 2009. It is my understanding that before this is completely over, 40 to 44 people in the county may be indicted. It seems to me that the rotten core of this corruption was based here in the Maple Heights City Schools.

They had a money scheme which affected not only the residents of Maple Heights, but spread throughout Cuyahoga County.

The school board President was charged with bribes, lying to the Feds, tax fraud and more. The Treasurer was listed as a public official on the indictment. The main attorney died, but two of his associates were also charged and indicted. The school Board's President's boss, the County Auditor, fits the description on the indictment, as public official number one. This was a wide spread scam that affected thousands of tax payers, businesses, and children, all for the 'love of money'. My parents always told me, "What's done in the dark, will one day come to the light". I have passed this on to my children to always do the right thing. I have a new found faith in our justice system. It does work if you just give it time and never give up!

References:

May 3, 1996 – Letter sent to the United States Department of Education, Re #15-96-1129

July 10, 1996 – Letters from United States Department of Education Re #15-96–1129

March 26, 2001 – Maple Heights Schools Pay Big Money for Lawyers Cleveland Plain Dealer, Page 3B

March 27, 2001 – Maple Heights Busy Lawyers Cleveland Plain Dealer, Page 8B

August 22, 2001 – Feds Asked For Help Cleveland Life Newspaper, Front Page 10-11

December 2002 – Critique Magazine School Board Removal Drive Continues

January 7, 2004 – New Magazine on School Board Sets Different Tune – Firing District Lawyer Cleveland Plain Dealer

July 9, 2009 – US Charges Outline Schemes Used to Get Jobs And Influence Cleveland Plain Dealer, Page A-4

August 23, 2009 – Controversy Surrounds Long Time Russo Loyalists Cleveland Plain Dealer, Front Page, A1

September 19, 2009 – Russo Aide Charged In $1.23 Million Bribery Scheme and Attorney Cleveland Plain Dealer, Front Page

September 30, 2009 – Lawyer Pleads Guilty to Bribery Charges in Auditor's Office Case Cleveland Plain Dealer, Page B-2

Never Give Up